Moe Berg

SPY CATCHER

by Jeri Cipriano
illustrated by Scott R. Brooks

RED
CHAIR
· PRESS ·

Hidden History: Spies is produced and published by Red Chair Press:

Red Chair Press LLC   PO Box 333   South Egremont, MA 01258-0333

www.redchairpress.com

Publisher's Cataloging-In-Publication Data

Names: Cipriano, Jeri S. | Brooks, Scott R., 1963- illustrator.

Title: Moe Berg : spy catcher / by Jeri Cipriano ; illustrated by Scott R. Brooks.

Description: [South Egremont, Massachusetts] : Red Chair Press, [2018] | Series: Hidden
    history: spies | Interest age level: 008-012. | Includes sidebars of interest, a glossary, and
    resources to learn more. | Includes bibliographical references and index. | Summary:
    "Some people call him the smartest baseball player of all time. Moe Berg could speak
    twelve languages -and make up signs on the baseball diamond. How did this major
    league catcher go on to become an American spy in World War II?"--Provided by
    publisher.

Identifiers: LCCN 2017933811 | ISBN 978-1-63440-280-4 (library hardcover) | ISBN 978-1-
    63440-286-6 (ebook)

Subjects: LCSH: Berg, Moe, 1902-1972--Juvenile literature. | Spies--United States--
    History--20th century--Juvenile literature. | World War, 1939-1945--Secret service-
    -United States--Juvenile literature. | CYAC: Berg, Moe, 1902-1972. | Spies--United
    States--History--20th century. | World War, 1939-1945--Secret service--United States.

Classification: LCC D810.S8 B47 2018 (print) | LCC D810.S8 (ebook) | DDC
    940.54/86/0924--dc23

Photo credit: p. 6: Jewish Baseball Museum; p. 9: Library of Congress; p. 28: Wikipedia
(public domain); p. 32: Courtesy of the author, Jeri Cipriano; p. 32: Courtesy of the
illustrator, Scott R. Brooks

Illustrations: p. 10, 15, 16: Joe LeMonnier

Printed in the United States of America

1117 1P CGBS18

Table of Contents

Chapter 1

The Call to Action

The year was 1934. The place was Tokyo, Japan. A man stood on the roof of a hospital. He was taking pictures of the buildings all around him. The Japanese were making war bombs in those buildings.

The man was an American ball player. Years later, Japan would bomb the United States. America would be at war with Japan. The man's photos would help the war effort.

Who was this man? Why did people call him the "smartest baseball player" of all time?

The man's name was Moe Berg. He played baseball for 15 years in the **major leagues**. He was a star **catcher**. Later, he would be a spy for the United States during **World War II**.

Baseball Code

Moe Berg had two loves: baseball and languages. In all, he knew twelve languages, including Greek and Latin. During games, Berg would call to his second baseman in Latin. The other team could never figure out his "code."

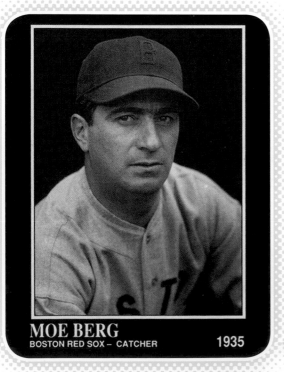

MOE BERG
BOSTON RED SOX – CATCHER   1935

Visiting Japan

In 1934, Berg was on a **goodwill tour** in Japan. American ball players had come to teach Japanese players how to play a better game of baseball. Berg traveled with an American All-Star team that included baseball greats, such as Babe Ruth and Lou Gehrig.

Berg loved languages almost as much as he loved baseball. Before the visit, he learned Japanese. He was able to speak to Japanese players in their own language.

In Japan, the U.S. team members stayed close together. Not Berg. He would often change his baseball uniform for a gray suit, white shirt, and black tie and slip away from the others.

One day he heard that the daughter of a U.S. ambassador had given birth in a Japanese hospital. He quickly changed his clothes for a Japanese *kimono* (a Japanese robe) and bought a bouquet of flowers. Berg went to the hospital, pretending to visit the new mother. Once inside, Berg threw away the flowers and climbed the stairs to the roof.

From Catcher to Spy

Think about it. Baseball catchers are *spies*. They "read" the field. They study the hitters. They gather intelligence. They make up signs. Moe Berg had the qualities of a good spy.

On the roof, Berg took out a movie camera from under his kimono. He took pictures of Japanese buildings. He had a feeling his photos might someday be useful.

Berg left the rooftop and slipped out of the hospital. He joined his teammates at dinner. They never realized he had been gone.

War Breaks Out

On December 7, 1941, Japan shocked the world by dropping bombs on U.S. ships near Hawaii. More than 2,000 American soldiers were killed.

The U.S. had no choice. President Franklin Roosevelt declared war. At the time, countries in Europe were fighting World War II. Countries like England and France were fighting a dangerous German leader named Adolph Hitler. Now the United States would be joining in the fight.

President Franklin Roosevelt

Call to Action

Moe Berg felt the "call to action." Berg was Jewish. He knew that Hitler and his **Nazi** government were killing millions of Jews. Berg wanted to help defeat him. Berg took his Japanese movie pictures to high **officials** in the U.S. government. He let them know he wanted to help.

Berg gave up baseball to work for the U.S. government. His first job was to travel through all of South and Central America. He visited 40 countries in all. When he returned, he knew which countries were friendly with Hitler and which were friends of the U.S.

Who was Moe Berg *really*? What inspired him to play pro ball? To learn twelve languages? What made him become a spy and risk his life during WW II? To find out, learn about Moe's life growing up.

Chapter 2

Moe Berg: The Early Years

Berg's parents were Russian Jews. Their families expected them to marry each other. They agreed, but on their own terms. Bernard Berg and Rose Tasker would marry in America.

Bernard traveled to America alone. On the trip, he taught himself to read English, French, and German. (He already knew Yiddish, Hebrew, and Russian.) In New York, he quickly learned to speak English. From that point on, he and his family would speak only English.

Rose joined Bernard in 1896. By then, Bernard was running his own laundry and taking classes at night to become a **pharmacist**.

The Bergs had three children. The youngest, Morris ("Moe" for short) was born in 1902. In 1906, the Bergs moved to Newark, New Jersey. They lived above their drugstore.

Parents would bring their sick children to see Bernard. If the symptoms were serious, Bernard told them to see a doctor. Otherwise, he'd treat the children himself. Bernard often did not charge poor families for prescriptions. The Bergs became an important part of their community.

School Days

Like his two older siblings, Moe did very well in school. But even as a toddler, he loved to play catch. He would beg his older brother Sam to play with him. They would toss apples and oranges back and forth.

As a boy, Moe played catch with a policeman neighbor. He'd run twenty feet down the street and stand behind a manhole. "Harder! Harder!" he would shout, as the policeman threw balls to him.

Setting Things Right

Berg's father didn't want Moe to play baseball. He wanted him to be a lawyer. To please his father, Berg went to law school in the off seasons. He got his law degree in 1930, but he never wanted to practice law.

Moe played baseball all through school. Along with baseball, he loved languages. He went on to Princeton University to study languages. At Princeton, he played **shortstop** on the baseball team. When he graduated in 1923, he was ready to play for the Brooklyn Dodgers[1].

---

[1]The team's name was the Brooklyn Robins when Moe first joined.

Play Ball!

Moe played shortstop for baseball teams for several years before he got his big break. In 1927, Moe was the shortstop for the Chicago White Sox. During one game, the catcher broke his hand. Then the backup catcher tore open his finger. Last, the third-string catcher fractured his finger. All in one game!

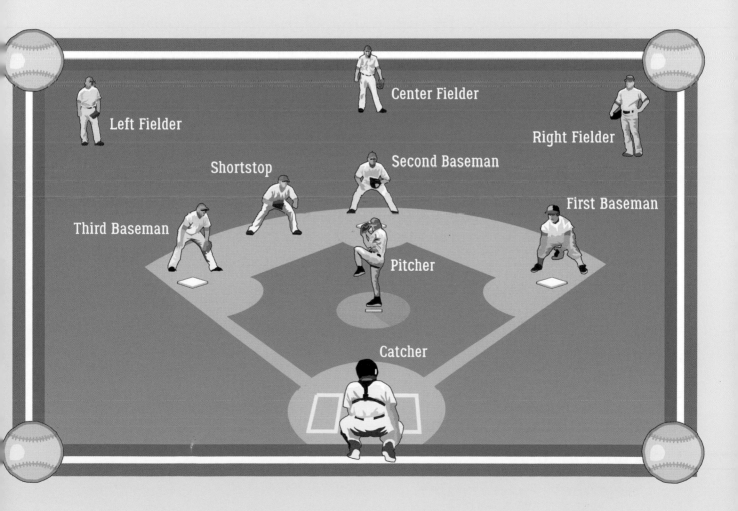

"A catcher! A catcher! Get us a catcher. Quick!" yelled the manager. Moe called back, "You've got a catcher sitting right here on the bench!" He was referring to a teammate who had been catcher for a minor league. The manager thought Moe was talking about himself. "Hurry up," he shouted. "Get ready. Suit up!"

Moe hadn't caught since his school days, yet he made no errors. In that game, Babe Ruth couldn't get a single hit. As for Moe, he found his rightful spot on the team. He was a catcher!

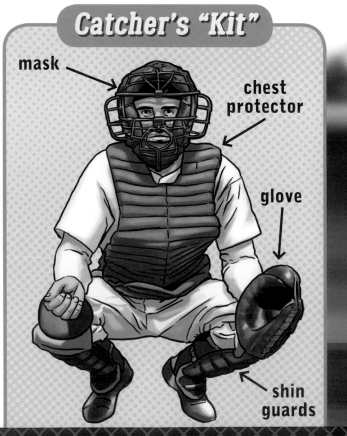

Catcher's "Kit"

mask

chest protector

glove

shin guards

Moe caught in nine more games that year. He had great hands and a strong arm. He studied the batters and learned their strengths and weaknesses. He used what he knew to call **signs**. Some say he knew where the batter was going to hit before the batter did. Pitchers felt **confident** when Moe was catching. What's more, his shortstop experience helped him pick up short hops that most catchers would miss.

Chapter 3

From Baseball to Spy Games

Berg's trip throughout Latin America for the U.S. government was a success. Now he was in line to do more important work. President Roosevelt needed to know more than what the FBI could tell him. He needed special agents.

Roosevelt established the first U.S. intelligence agency. It was called the OSS[2] for short. Later, it would be known as the CIA[3]. Berg was one of the first spies to come on board. He was smart. He knew many languages. He liked to travel. He could blend into any group—and secretly "fade out" or "blend in."

---

[2] Office of Strategic Services
[3] Central Intelligence Agency

Getting in Shape

Spring training for pro ball is hard. Training to be a spy is harder. Moe learned how to use guns and blow up bridges. He learned how to pick locks and crack open safes. He learned how to fight with his hands and jump out of planes.

Top Secret!

Moe worked on top secret projects. One plan was so top-secret that not even the vice president knew about it.

Scientists around the world were trying to make a powerful bomb. This bomb could blow up an entire city. Germany bragged that they had such a weapon. It was Moe's job to find out if their boasting was true.

Nazis on Trial

As a spy, Berg was learning more about German cruelty to Jews. He kept his own list of top Nazi officials who were responsible. After the war, he helped bring these men to justice. He was in the court when the men were convicted of war crimes.

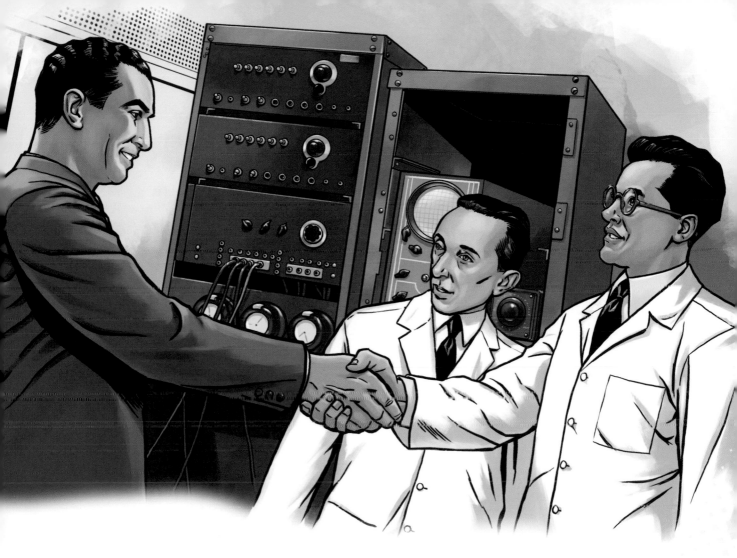

Moe had to "become" a scientist. He had to learn everything scientists knew. Then he had to meet with scientists and figure out how close they were to building an **atomic bomb**.

Moe had to sneak into Italy and persuade Italian scientists to come help the U.S. They traveled undercover by submarine. The Italian scientists would help the U.S. find the German scientists who were working on the bomb.

English and German secret agents wanted the Italian scientists too, but Berg got to them first. One scientist he met was working on high-speed flight.

Berg knew the country with the fastest planes could win the war. England and Germany were rushing to build **supersonic** airplanes. No time to waste! Berg smuggled the scientist out of Italy. Now the U.S. could build supersonic planes to help win the war.

Honors from Italy

To thank Moe for the kindness he had shown all the Italian scientists, the president of Italy gave Moe an honorary degree as Doctor of Law from the University of Rome.

Chapter 4

A Dangerous Mission

Nearly two years had passed since he started working with the Italian scientists. Berg was still on the trail of Werner Heisenberg. Germany was depending on this man to make the atom bomb. Berg had orders to kill the scientist to keep Germany from winning the war with this weapon.

Berg had to get Heisenberg out of Germany to get a shot at him. Berg, too, had to be ready to die. Every spy carried a poison pill to swallow. If caught, he'd die and take all secrets with him.

Berg persuaded the Swiss to invite Heisenberg to give a lecture in Switzerland, which was a safe place to meet. Berg pretended to be a "student" at the lecture. He hoped Heisenberg would talk about the atomic bomb, but he didn't. What to do? If he shot Heisenberg, he would not leave the room alive either.

Werner Heisenberg

The First "Spy Master"

George Washington used spies to win the American Revolution. He knew he couldn't out-fight Great Britain. He'd have to "out spy" them. With fewer soldiers than Britain, General Washington had to know exactly where to put them to win the war.

Berg knew the war was not going well for Germany. He had a hunch that Germany did not yet have the bomb. If they did, he reasoned, they would have used it by now.

When Heisenberg left the room, Berg left also. Berg pretended to be walking the same way. Pretty soon the two men were speaking. The conversation made Berg stick with his gut instinct. He let Heisenberg get away.

Into Enemy Territory

The war was coming to an end. Germany had lost. Now U.S. troops could move into Germany. Berg was right with them. He had to see where scientists were making the atom bomb. When Berg found the lab, he was shocked. There was nothing inside. All along, Germany's bragging had been a big lie. Berg's instincts had been right!

At Peace

After the war, Moe did not take a job as a lawyer or a coach. Instead, he waited for a "call to action." He knew the **Cold War** between Russia and the United States had begun. He wanted to get the inside story on the Russians.

He kept in shape by running. He kept writing fresh ideas in his spy notebook. But the new CIA never called. Moe went back to his first love. He traveled to Princeton to watch baseball games. And he was often seen sitting with reporters in the press box at White Sox games.

Moe Berg died on May 29th, 1972. His last words were: "How are the Mets doing today?"

The Country's Highest Honor

In 1945, Moe was awarded the Medal of Freedom. For a U.S. citizen, it is the highest honor. The medal could not state any specific act of heroism. Berg was also sworn to secrecy. To everyone's surprise, Berg returned the medal. He said it embarrassed him.

"Maybe I'm not in the Cooperstown Baseball Hall of Fame like so many of my baseball buddies, but I'm happy I had the chance to play pro ball and am especially proud of my contributions to my country."

Glossary

atomic bomb highly destructive bomb that uses nuclear energy

catcher the player behind home plate who catches pitched balls; also catches balls from fielders to make "outs" at home plate.

Cold War an unfriendly relationship between nations not officially at war

confident feeling good about your own abilities

goodwill friendly feelings

major leagues the highest-ranking leagues in baseball

Nazi members of the Nazi (National Socialists) Party reported to Hitler and carried out his plans

officials people who have important jobs

pharmacist a trained person who prepares and sells medicines

shortstop a baseball player who stands between second and third base.

sign a signal that stands for something

supersonic very fast speeds of almost 2,500 miles per hour.

tour when a team goes on tour, it travels to a place to play and teach

World War II a war in which the United States, France, Great Britain, the Soviet Union, and other nations defeated Germany, Italy, and Japan. World War II started in 1939 when Germany invaded Poland and ended in 1945 with the surrender of Germany and Japan.

For More Information

Books

Briggs, Andy. *How to Be an International Spy: Your top secret guide to international espionage.* Lonely Planet Kids, 2015.

Cieradkowski, Gary Joseph. *The League of Outsider Baseball: An illustrated guide to baseball's forgotten heroes.* Touchstone, Simon and Schuster, 2015.

Earnest, Peter with Suzanne Harper. *The Real Spy's Guide to Becoming a Spy.* Abrams, 2009.

Web Sites

Jewish Baseball Museum

http://jewishbaseballmuseum.com/?s=Moe+berg

CIA Kids Zone

https://www.cia.gov/kids-page

Places

Baseball Hall of Fame, Cooperstown, NY.

Index

About the Author and Illustrator

Jeri Cipriano has been a children's writer and editor for many years. She is the author of more than 100 books and served as an editorial director of classroom magazines at Scholastic. When Jeri is not writing, she enjoys taking photographs of people and places.

Scott R. Brooks started a career in full-time illustration several years ago. Scott shares his Atlanta, GA studio with his illustrator wife, Karen. They share their home with their 2 clever children, and their somewhat less clever dog and cat.